Animals and the Seasons

The Cycle of Nature

Susanne Riha

BLACKBIRCH PRESS, INC.
WOODBRIDGE, CONNECTICUT

Published by Blackbirch Press, Inc.
260 Amity Road
Woodbridge, CT 06525
web site: http://www.blackbirch.com
e-mail: staff@blackbirch.com

© 2000 Blackbirch Press, Inc.
First Edition

All rights reserved. No part of this book may be reproduced in any form without permission in writing from Blackbirch Press, Inc., except by a reviewer.

Printed in Belgium

10 9 8 7 6 5 4 3 2 1

First published in German as *Mein erstes Buch vom ganzen Jahr* by Annette Betz Verlag, © 1999.

Translated by Charlotte Sanford.

Library of Congress Cataloging-in-Publication Data
Riha, Susanne.
 [Mein erstes buch vom ganzen jahr. English].
 Animals and the seasons: the cycle of nature / Susanne Riha.—1st ed.
   p. cm.
 "A blackbirch nature book."
 Summary: Discusses how the habits and life cycles of some animals such as foxes, swans, prairie dogs, and others change during each season.
 ISBN 1-56711-429-6
 Library Catalog Card Number 99-059475

Contents

January	6
February	8
March	10
April	12
May	14
June	16
July	18
August	20
September	22
October	24
November	26
December	28
Glossary	30
For More Information	30
Index	30

January

January is always one of winter's coldest months. A layer of shimmering white frost covers everything in the valley. A cold north wind blows the bare branches of maple and elm trees. It is very cold in the mountains; the brooks and the waterfalls even freeze there. On some days, fresh snow falls from the thick, flat clouds. This blanket of snow can get very deep. Many ponds and lakes are frozen with thick layers of ice.

Grass and bushes have small snowcaps. In hollow stems, insects and spiders lie still, waiting for winter to end. Most trees are bare. Only the nests of the squirrels and a few abandoned bird's nests hang between exposed branches. The trees, like most animals, also have a winter's rest: they don't grow now. But, since the summer, they have been wearing buds that await the springtime sun. Spruces and fir trees have stayed green. A wax layer protects their needles from the cold.

What is there to discover in January?

At night, deer, squirrels, hares, foxes, and other animals come out in search of food. In fresh snow, their tracks can be seen. They search for hay, chestnuts, acorns, and nuts.

Many animals go to sleep (hibernate) for the winter. To prepare, woodchucks and deer mice almost double their weight during the fall. Now they lie in a ball and sleep until spring. During this time, their body temperature drops greatly. A deer mouse has filled his underground house with grains. He wakes up regularly during the winter months to eat from his stash. Between the soil and the snow cover, field mice have burrowed a network of tunnels. Hungry, they search from one end to the other, looking for leftover plants.

A nearby ermine is one animal that is not sleeping. Covered by a warm winter coat, he scurries around in search of food above ground. Against the snow, his white fur makes him hard to see. Only the tip of his tail is black. During the summer he is reddish-brown. The ermine doesn't run, he jumps. His hind paws always spring right up next to the front paws. Because of this, the tracks of this animal are a double row of tiny holes. The area's field mice have to watch out for this member of the weasel family. An ermine is a clever hunter. With his sharp senses, he scouts, listens, and sniffs around in the snow for food.

WINTER

February

February is the sunniest of the three winter months. It is still snowy, but the days slowly grow longer. By the end of the month, some things will begin to thaw out. The thick blanket of snow covering the ground begins to melt. When the winter air becomes moist, tiny water droplets form on branches and grasses. Sometimes these water droplets freeze and a white frost forms, making the buildings, trees, and shrubs look like they are covered with sugar.

As the snow melts, patches of ground can be seen in the forest. Here, the first snowdrops, crocuses, and daffodils bloom. Hazelnut trees are one of the first trees to bloom for the year.

Small catkins, or flower clusters, have sat on the branches of the hazelnut trees since last summer. At the end of the month, catkins will change into little sausage-shaped pods and begin to give off pollen to fertilize the hazelnut trees. The nuts will be ripe by the end of August.

What is there to discover in February?

Spider webs, with their threads coated by white frost, are easy to spot. But spiders crawl into cracks in trees, or into folded-up leaves, to protect themselves from the cold.

During the winter, animals move as little as possible in order to conserve their energy. Badgers rest curled up in their dens. Rabbits and hares let themselves be slightly snowed into their holes, which are called warrens.

The best place to see wildlife is around birdfeeders. These feeding stations are buzzing with activity. They usually attract many different types of birds because the containers are full of dried berries, seeds, raisins, oatmeal, and wheat kernels. Sparrows prefer to eat oatmeal. Green finches pick kernels out of rosehips. Robins like raisins. Some of the birds squawk and squeak as they flutter and fight for room to perch.

Suet rings hang under the roofs of some birdfeeders for titmice, nuthatches, and woodpeckers.

Titmice will also hold sunflower seeds tightly in their claws and hammer the shells open with their beaks to expose the seeds inside. Beneath the birdfeeder, thrushes discover pieces of apple on the ground and fly away with them. Jays hop through the snow, seeking the acorns and beechnuts that they collected and buried last fall. Once they are dug up, these nuts become a tasty winter meal.

WINTER

March

By the beginning of March, much of the valley has thawed. The nights are still quite cold and the mornings are foggy and frosty. The air is moist and chilling. But every day the sun appears earlier than it had the day before. And each day, the fog burns off more quickly as the crisp air turns clear. The mountains are also becoming warmer. Water gushes into the valley through wild-running streams fed by the melting mountain snow.

As soon as the frost has passed, the first leaves and buds show themselves. The meadows quickly become green. And the forest air smells of onion grass and skunk cabbage. Liverwort, wood anemone, and primrose shoot up from under the forest floor. They are warmed by sunlight—the canopy of leaves above them has not yet grown too thick. On the edge of the forest, the first bees visit the yellow willow cattails. And the dogwood branches pop out their first buds.

What is there to discover in March?

The skylark is one of the first migrating birds to return from the south. The female bird builds her nest on the ground. The male bird flies in small circles up to 330 feet (101 meters) high, singing the entire time.

In March, most male birds begin looking for a mate. In some forests, the woodpecker drums a hollow trunk, calling for a female. The male blue titmouse feeds his mate in the hedges. On the pond, the drake and the duck are always together. They remain a couple for life.

As the sun warms the air, a woodchuck awakens from his deep winter sleep. He and the snake warm themselves on sunny rocks or fallen tree trunks. Well-hidden in the underbrush, wild piglets have been born. The young will be nursed for three months by their mother, the sow. They can already accompany her in search of food. Peccaries dig in the ground for worms, insects, and roots. By autumn, the young boars will have lost their striped coats. A jackrabbit has also already given birth. Her babies come into the world completely covered with hair. When mother leaves their hollow in the ground to go out searching for food, the young crouch motionless, huddled together. Their fur is as brown as the earth around them. The babies are well-camouflaged and don't yet have a body smell, so they are not easily noticed by foxes, wolves, eagles, or hawks.

SPRING

April

April's weather is changeable. First, it may rain. Then the sun may shine before it snows a little. Suddenly, hail may tumble from a dark cloud. Soon, the hail may pass and a strong wind may begin to blow.

By the end of the month, days are mostly filled with rain. The April air has also become quite a bit warmer. Now, whenever it rains and the sun shines afterward, a rainbow appears in the moist air.

For the plants in the meadows and the valleys, spring has finally arrived in full. In the backyard, cherry trees, dogwoods, and currant bushes begin to bloom. Flowerbeds overflow with tulips and daffodils. The meadows have been sown with dandelions and, on the riverbanks, wild grasses bloom. In the forest, arum blooms; its scent attracts a swarm of buzzing flies and swiftly crawling beetles.

What is there to discover in April?
A ladybug scurries across a branch. Like many other insects, it has survived the winter living in a tree crack. Now the ladybug will lay her eggs and go off in search of aphids and other food. An adult ladybug can eat up to 100 aphids a day.

In other parts of the trees, many birds are sitting on their eggs. The blackbirds already have young. The pond on the edge of the forest is now full of frogs and toads. A chorus of "spring peepers" croaks in pulsing rhythms. The first to arrive were the toads. They wander here each year to mate and lay their sticky eggs (spawn) near or in the water. The smaller male toads let the larger female toads carry them to the water. When the female spawns, she wraps a 3-foot- (1meter) long strand of egg jelly around the stems of nearby waterplants. The grass frog also uses the pond as a place to deposit its eggs. During the rest of the year, the toads live far away from the water. Now their spawn floats in clumps, bobbing gently on the water's surface.

The swamp and pond are noisy all night. Treefrogs croak the loudest, because only they have a throat sac outside of their throat. They can blow this special sac up to the size of their own body. By the time treefrogs finally attach their eggs to the water plants, thousands of tiny toad tadpoles will have already hatched. As soon as they are free, they wriggle through the water in search of food.

SPRING

May

During May there are many warm, sunny days with little or no wind. The spring air is often clear and dry. It can still get cold once or twice more in the mountains, however. There, it is likely to rain almost twice as much as in the valleys. Despite a few snaps of cold weather, the sun shines in May for about seven or eight hours per day. It warms the air even more quickly now, and the nights don't cool down as much.

May is the month for blossoms: apple trees, pear trees, and lilacs bloom. Horsechestnuts produce white or pink candle-like blossoms. Red catchflys, yellow buttercups, and blue meadow sage light up the fields. Bumblebees fly from clover to clover. Only bumblebees, with their long proboscises (tube-like snouts), can draw nectar out of the narrow clover heads. These hairy insects carry pollen from one plant to the next. This is how blossoms are pollinated.

What is there to discover in May?

Lilies of the valley bloom in large clumps throughout the woods. Often, many are tangled thickly together. Lilies of the valley shouldn't be picked—they are poisonous.

Now female cuckoos lay their eggs in the nests they have stolen from other birds. The moment a nest is unprotected, a cuckoo will quickly take possession. Cuckoos are particularly fond of nests built by wrens, robins, or reed warblers. A cuckoo's egg is only a little bit larger than the eggs from those birds. When the first young cuckoo hatches, the first thing it does is push the other eggs out of the nest. That means only one cuckoo is raised and fed by the parents.

Two kits (young foxes) roughhouse near their den. A third has discovered a dead mouse. He crouches, sneaks around, and springs on his prey. The small foxes are already three months old, but they have only been able to play outside for a few days now. Foxes are blind at birth and covered in a gray, wooly coat. Later, their eyes turn dark blue. After 5 weeks, the young foxes' eyes change to an amber color and their coat changes to orange. Finally, a mother fox returns home from her search for food. She brings her kits a meal. She steps through the snow with a dead mouse she has captured. She approaches her den in a zigzag path so that watchful predators won't be able to follow her easily.

SPRING

June

Most days in June are long and bright. The sun's rays warm the air and the earth. Even the nights now are comfortably warm with a fresh, cooling breeze. It is during this month that spring finally shifts into summer. On the 21st of June, the sun reaches its apex (highest arc) and creates the longest day of the year. During this time—called the summer solstice—it can be light for up to 16 hours a day.

During the night, an orb-weaving spider has spun her web into an insect trap. She wants to be ready because many plants—such as sweet pea or dogwood—open their blossoms very early in the morning. There is buzzing in the hedges and treetops. The bees have much to do. Lime trees and acacia are in full bloom. In June, grasses and grains have also flowered. Fine pollen whirls through the air, dusting leaves and branches everywhere.

What is there to discover in June?

In the warm June evening a small light appears on a branch. It is a "June bug," or a firefly. A firefly is actually a beetle that can create light with the tail end of his body. The unique flashing pattern of his light is used to attract a mate.

The lake shimmers in the sun. An emperor dragonfly whirs like a helicopter through the air. A long-legged waterstrider scurries over the lake's surface. A green-headed mallard flies above his mate and young as he approaches a clump of duckweed. A group of recently hatched mute swans hops a ride on the back of their large, white mother. The babies have been learning how to search for food in the water. After a long lesson, they are tired, so their mother takes them upon her back and carries them for a while. At this young age, the cygnets (baby swans) are completely gray and their beaks are black. After a half year, they will grow their brown adolescent feathers. After four years, they will be fully grown. At this age, their feathers will be entirely white. When they are in the water, the young swans do headstands, exactly as their parents do. This is how they learn to dive down to snatch the many delicious plants that grow on the bottom of the lake. Swans have a special "tooth" on the tips of their upper beaks that helps them to break off the weeds they find. As they grow into adulthood, they will become expert weed gatherers.

SUMMER

July

July is usually the sunniest month of the year. But during this time, heat and moisture build up in the air. Clumps of dark, thick clouds warn of heavy storms approaching. From inside the clouds, huge bolts of lightning emerge, filling the sky with flashes of bright white light. A few seconds go by. Now thunder rumbles low and then explodes into a booming clap. The noise shakes the ground in vibration.

Currant and blueberry bushes, peach and cherry trees all hang with round, ripe fruit. Bellflowers, daisies, thistle, bluebells, and clover fill the rolling fields with blooms.

Everywhere, crickets are chirping loudly. To attract a mate, a male cricket rubs his wings together. The edge of one wing strokes a row of tiny teeth on the edge of the other wing. As the wings rub, a chirping sound is made. After chirping, one cricket disappears into his hole in the earth, digging deeper by vibrating his body.

In July, young storks and many other birds will fledge (fly for the first time). Together with their parents, they flap their wings and take their first journeys. From above, a kestrel uses her keen eyesight to patrol the fields below. She catches up to 30 mice a day and brings them back to her nest. She has many hungry baby birds waiting there. Busy butterflies also seek nourishment in the summer. Monarchs and swallow-tails suck nectar out of flowers.

A young grasshopper bounces by. He can't fly yet, but he can jump quite well. He takes a giant leap when the earth underneath him suddenly heaves. A mole is digging underground. With his wide, turned-out paws, he digs and tunnels, pushing earth out of his way. His large, flat paws act like shovels underground. The mole is almost blind, but he senses every vibration around him. Something makes him stop suddenly. He turns and digs a new path, this time finding a rich supply of grubs or worms. A mole can dig forward and backward. Some days, he digs tunnels as long as 60 feet (18 meters).

What is there to discover in July?

The first wild strawberries are ripe in a sunny place on the edge of the woods. Wild strawberries have white blossoms, but the berries are much smaller than those grown on fruit farms.

SUMMER

August

Temperatures can rise very high in August. It can be hot and humid for many days in a row. And there is little relief from a breeze. Some farmers use this dry period to harvest grains from their fields. It is even warm in the mountains. August is also an especially beautiful time to view the summer sunset in the clear air. Now "high summer" draws to an end. Towards the end of the month, the nights are already noticeably cooler.

Farmers will spend their days harvesting oats and wheat after the rye and barley are in. Some fields will be mowed for the second time in the year. The dried hay will be winter food for the cows. On the edge of the fields, a farmer will leave a border. Here, between the wild herbs, grow larkspur, camomile, thistle, and the last corn poppies. Toward the end of the month, the first meadow saffron appears on the damp meadows.

What is there to discover in August?
The sunflowers are now blooming. Their large blossoms always turn to face the direction of the sun. In the morning, they bow toward the east, and during the day, they turn toward the west.

On hot days, even the animals like to take a bath. Birds bathe in puddles—peccaries and white-tailed deer prefer to lay down in muddy water. Later, the dried mud on their coats protects them from irritating mosquitoes. When the sun goes down, a harvest mouse peeps out of her round nest. She has cleverly woven rolled leaves between the stalks of high grains and grasses. For the third time this summer, the harvest mouse has given birth to many babies.

The tiny harvest mouse climbs nimbly and swings herself gracefully through the stalks. She eats mostly the grain from the plants around her, but also enjoys dining on insects and small fruits.

In the evenings, a deer mouse leaves his underground sleeping chamber. He strains his ears to listen around him, then he runs out. A partridge is also searching for grain. Quickly, the deer mouse stuffs his cheeks full of grain and scurries back to his house. In his supply chamber, next to his sleeping chamber, he presses the grain out of his cheeks with his paws. By late autumn, the mouse will have collected enough food to last through a long winter.

SUMMER

September

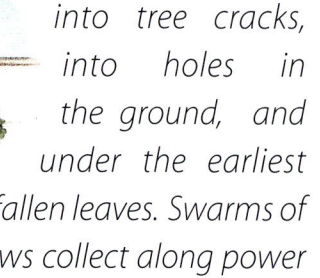

Many days in September are still comfortably warm—and the sky is bright blue. But in the fields and meadows it has already become more still. As the nights become colder and damper, many insects crawl into tree cracks, into holes in the ground, and under the earliest fallen leaves. Swarms of swallows collect along power lines to gather warmth. Like many migrating birds, the swallows are now ready to fly south.

In September, pears, plums, hazelnuts, and horsechestnuts ripen. For the last time this year, the birds will feast. Bushes are weighed down with rosehips, elderberries, blackberries, and late raspberries. The seeds from these plants will be scattered in the birds' droppings. This is how these trees and shrubs spread. Alpine clematis and dandelions, among others, will allow their seeds to be carried by the wind.

What is there to discover in September?
A day or so after a downpour, mushrooms shoot out of the forest floor. But be careful! Many of them, like the sparkling red fly agaric, are poisonous. They are fun to find, but don't touch!

It is not yet cold in the mountains. But the buck and the mountain goat have already begun their descent from the peaks. Skillfully, they climb over the cliff walls and jump over deep crevices. The animals are heading for the woods. There, they can find enough food and protection for the long winter ahead.

A group of prairie dogs is on the move in September. Plump and well fed, they leave their summer house in the meadow and wander toward the valley. Together, they dig a hole in the hillside. Soon small passages are completed—they lead to a large living chamber. The animals pad the chamber with dried blades of grass and other soft plants.

The prairie dogs keep a close eye out while working. One may even stand guard. With his sharp eyes, he spots a distant eagle in the sky. When danger threatens, he whistles loudly. Quickly, all the prairie dogs disappear underground. Soon they all withdraw into their well-cushioned burrow. Each family, or group, has its own chamber connected to all the other chambers by long, winding tunnels. They block their entrances and snuggle close together as they sleep away the months to come.

FALL

October

Now the days are growing shorter more quickly. It is getting colder, too. In the mountains, rain storms are more common, and the first snow falls. During the day, the sun no longer sits high in the sky.

Now, the rays stream sideways into the forest and do not warm the trees and plants very well. The leaves on many trees have already changed their colors. Some have fallen to the forest floor.

In the beginning of October the acorns, beechnuts, and walnuts are ripe. Slowly their leaves change colors as well. First go the chestnut and beech. Shortly thereafter follow the birch, maple, and oak. At the very end of the season, the ash changes colors. The wind whirls the wilted leaves off the branches. Soon the forest floor is covered with a thick mat of wet, colored leaves.

What is there to discover in October?

The larch is the only coniferous tree whose needles change color in the fall. Its needles turn yellow and drop to the ground. The larch can grow up to 120 feet (37 meters) tall. Its wood is especially hard.

In October, snails dig themselves into the loose ground. Then they close up their shells with a lime covering. Frogs, toads, and salamanders are also in search of winter quarters. When it is rainy and cold, the nearby red ants close up the air passageways of their anthill. A tawny owl spends the day in a hole of a tree. At night, he flies silently through the woods. With keen eyes and ears, he searches the ground for mice and chipmunks. When he spots one, he will swoop in and grab his prey with great precision.

During October, elk stags start staying close to the does. Each stag attempts to round up for himself as many does as possible. In order to protect his herd, he roars loudly. When another stag approaches, the males will fight. With their powerful antlers, they will push and shove each other until the weaker one becomes injured, gives up, or runs away.

A doe is pregnant for eight months. Only in the spring will she bear young. During its first weeks, a calf will have a white-spotted back. It will nurse from its mother during the entire summer and into autumn. Only then will it feed itself from the leaves, bark, and fruits it finds on its daily search for food.

FALL

November

November is often a cold and rainy month. Some days are filled with fog, sleet, or wet snow. A gusty wind may blow. But it can still get warm again in November. Sometimes, a moist wind will blow in from the south and will remain for a few days. If it has come from across the plains, the wind will be even warmer. If this happens, clouds will build up over the mountains. In a couple of days, it will begin to pour.

The golden hues of October have now dulled into a dark gray landscape. Few leaves remain on the trees. Only the ivy stays green for the entire year. Burrs and thorns cling to the fur of wandering animals and are carried along. The leaves of past years are buried under the freshly fallen leaves of this year. They have decayed greatly. Slowly, small insects—woodlice, mites, or centipedes—eat their way through the rotten leftover leaves and help them to decompose.

What is there to discover in November?
On the treetrunks and stones there are strange growths. These are lichens. A lichen is a combination of fungi and algae. The fungi form the outside and the algae sits inside.

A worm fertilizes and plows the forest floor. She digs down through the damp, cool soil. When the rain fills the passageways with water, the worm comes to the surface. The body of the worm is separated into sections by many rings. These rings have many tiny crevices. The worm moves by stretching and contracting its ringed body sections. If the body of the worm gets torn apart, the longer part will eventually regrow the missing, shorter part.

A flock of crows has landed on the field. They are looking for insects, worms, and kernels to pick up in their sharp beaks. In the late afternoon the birds return to their meeting point. Hundreds of crows can gather here. Together, they fly to a main gathering point, where other large groups will join them. Through the evening they meet even more groups of birds that have arrived to join the flock. They all fly off and land again. Finally, before darkness falls completely, a flock of thousands of crows lifts itself up in unison to fly to the safety of a common sleeping place. The frenzied flapping of wings and the rough cawing of the birds can be heard for many miles in every direction.

FALL

December

In December, the cold air numbs your face and hands. There is little sunshine. On the 22nd of December—the shortest day of the year—the sun shines for only 6 or 7 hours. By late afternoon, it is already completely dark. A thin blanket of snow lies on the fields and in the city parks. Around Christmas, there can be one more deep thaw. After that, the coldest and harshest weather will begin.

The seed cones from coniferous trees (evergreens) actually ripen in the winter. More and more cones fall to the earth. In between the bare branches of deciduous trees (which lose their leaves), a small round bush is growing. It is mistletoe. Mistletoe is a parasitic plant. It digs its roots under the bark of another tree and nourishes itself from the sap. During the winter, mistletoe has white, sticky berries. Many people hang mistletoe over their doors as a Christmas decoration.

What is there to discover in December?

Upon a twig hangs a small butterfly. He seems as if he is frozen in ice. This is how the anglewing butterfly survives the winter. When spring arrives, the sun will wake him again.

A magpie flies through the city park. Often it will find something delicious in the garbage. The pond in the park has not yet frozen over. A flock of black-headed gulls has arrived here. Park visitors, bundled up warmly, help to feed them. The black-headed gulls now wear their winter coats of feathers as well.

A squirrel has left the comfort and safety of its nest—called a dray—in a nearby elm tree. He jumps from limb to limb. Often he jumps up to 12 feet (4 meters) at once. With his long claws, the squirrel can run down the tree head first. Now he jumps through the wet snow looking for food. All of a sudden, he stops in one place. Quickly, he digs down to retrieve a small stash of acorns and nuts he had buried in the ground during the fall. Finally, he discovers a pine cone. With his long front teeth he takes it apart piece by piece. Nervous and hungry, the squirrel eats the seeds that lie underneath. At its end, the pine cone has been completely peeled apart. Once the squirrel has filled his stomach, he scampers back to his warm nest high above the ground and sleeps several days away.

WINTER

Glossary

Canopy a protective covering.

Conserve to save something from loss or waste.

Fertilize when male sperm joins with female eggs to create a new beginning of life.

Hibernate to spend the winter in a deep sleep to survive low temperatures and lack of food.

Hollow empty in the center.

Migrate to move from one region or climate to another at a certain time of year or stage in life.

Nectar a sweet liquid that bees collect from flowers and turn into honey.

Nourish to provide food and care so something will grow and prosper.

Pollinate to transfer pollen from the stamen to the pistil of a flower so that the cell can be fertilized and produce seeds.

Precision the accuracy with which something is done.

Predator an animal that catches and eats other animals.

Prey an animal that is hunted by another animal for food.

Proboscis a long, tube-like snout of some insects that allows them to extract nectar or pollen from some plants.

Sow to scatter seed upon the earth to create new plants.

Stash something stored or hidden away.

Suet a hardened fat from cattle or sheep that some birds like to eat.

Thaw to melt after being frozen.

For More Information

Books

Bennett, Paul. *Hibernation* (Nature's Secrets). Chatham, NJ: Raintree/Steck Vaughn, 1996.

Fowler, Allan. *Animals Underground* (Rookie Read-About Series). Danbury, CT: Children's Press, 1997.

Livingston, Myra Cohn. Leonard Everett Fisher (Illustrator). *A Circle of Seasons*. New York, NY: Holiday House, 1992.

Orr, Richard. Shaila Awan. *The Burrow Book*. New York, NY: DK Publishing, 1997.

Simon, Seymour. *Ride the Wind: Airborne Journeys of Animals and Plants*. Orlando, FL: Harcourt Brace, 1997.

Simon, Seymour. Elsa Warnick (Illustrator). *They Swim the Seas: The Mystery of Animal Migration*. Orlando, FL: Browndeer Press, 1998.

Web Sites

All About Birds

Discover the migration patterns, characteristics, and cycles of life for various kinds of birds—www.enchantedlearning.com/subjects/birds/Birdwatching.com

Exploratorium: Frogs!

Through on-line exhibits, learn about the evolution, life cycle, and behavior of different species of frogs—www.exploratorium.edu/frogs

Index

Birdfeeders, 8, 9
Bumblebee, 14, 16

Cricket, 18
Crow, 26, 27
Cuckoo, 14

Daffodil, 8, 12
Deer, 24, 25
Deer mouse, 6
Dogwood, 10, 12
Dragonfly, 16

Ermine, 6, 7

Finches, 8
Firefly, 16
Fox, 14, 15
Frog, 12, 13, 24

Grasshopper, 18, 19
Gull, 28

Harvest mouse, 20, 21
Hibernation, 6

Kestrel, 18

Ladybug, 12

Lichen, 26

Mistletoe, 28
Mole, 18, 19
Mountain goat, 22
Mushroom, 22

Owl, 24

Peccary, 10
Prairie dog, 22, 23

Rabbit, 8, 10

Snail, 24
Spider, 16
Squirrel, 28, 29
Strawberry, 18
Sunflower, 20
Swan, 16, 17

Titmouse, 8, 9
Toads, 12, 13
Trees, 6, 14, 24

Woodchuck, 10
Worm, 26